ABOUT

Seth Tobocman has been drawing comic books about serious issues for three decades. He founded the political comic book *World War 3 Illustrated* in 1980 with Peter Kuper. Tobocman's books include *You Don't Have to Fuck People Over to Survive*, *War in the Neighborhood*, *Portraits of Israelis and Palestinians*, and *Disaster and Resistance*.

Louisa Krupp

Eric Laursen is an independent journalist and activist with an extensive background in financial and public-affairs reporting. His work has appeared in *The Village Voice* and *The Nation*, among other publications.

Jess Wehrle's work can also be seen in *Disaster and Resistance*, *The Bush Junta: A Field Guide to Corruption in Government*, and the upcoming epic *Return to Crunch Island*, among other titles.

Brian Volkert

UNDERSTANDING THE
CRASH

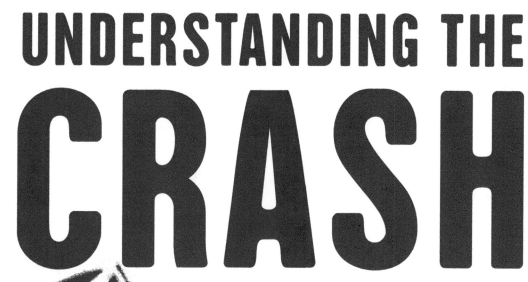

BY **SETH TOBOCMAN,**

ERIC LAURSEN, AND

JESSICA WEHRLE

FOREWORD BY

**DOUG
HENWOOD**

soft skull press • an imprint of
COUNTERPOINT BERKELEY

Library of Congress Cataloging-in-Publication Data
Tobocman, Seth.
   Understanding the crash / Seth Tobocman, Eric Laursen, and Jessica Wehrle;
introduction by Doug Henwood.
        p. cm.
   Includes bibliographical references and index.
   ISBN-13: 978-1-59376-272-8 (alk. paper)
1. Financial crises—United States. 2. United States—Economic conditions—
2001–2009. 3. Global Financial Crisis, 2008-2009. I. Laursen, Eric. II. Wehrle,
Jessica. III. Title.

   HB3722.T63 2010
   330.973'0931—dc22
                                    2010007182

Cover art by Seth Tobocman
Cover design by Aaron Artessa
Interior art by Seth Tobocman
Interior typesetting by Janine Agro, Neuwirth & Associates, Inc.
Printed in the United States of America

Soft Skull Press
An Imprint of Counterpoint LLC
1140 Broadway, Suite 704
New York, NY 10001

www.softskull.com
www.counterpointpress.com

Distributed by Publishers Group West

10 9 8 7 6 5 4

Dedicated to our grandparents, who were witness, to the Great Depression:
Helen Tobocman, Jacob Tobocman, Frida Perloff, Aaron Perloff,
Rosemary Wehrle, Maryjane Finlay, Tage Laursen, Dagmar Jensen Laursen,
Harold Sherwin, and Edna Crow Sherwin

(Above: portrait of Helen Tobocman, painted by Seth Tobocman, 1975)

TABLE OF CONTENTS

As I'm writing this, in January 2010, it's looking like the worst of the financial crisis is over and the real economy is staging a recovery—a very weak one, though. My guess is that the economy, which for most people means the job market, will stink for quite a while, perhaps years, so the difference between recession and recovery may seem academic to both the unemployed trying to find a job and the employed trying to make ends meet. Still, it's better than things falling totally apart, which is the way it felt at the beginning of 2009.

Yet despite the worst financial and economic troubles since the Great Depression, Americans seem to have learned almost nothing from their economic brush with death. At the elite level, the response has mainly been to spend enormous wads of public money on trying to restore the *status quo ante bustum*. There's been almost no effort to reform finance, which would require reregulating it in a serious way to avoid future catastrophes. In fact, in early 2010, it looks like Wall Street has gone back to business as usual. In a truly strange historical irony, Paul Volcker, one of the engineers of "The Great Crackdown" described in the chapter of the same title, is now being identified as the avatar of a new populism—a toothless effort to reregulate the banks driven more by the Obama administration's political desperation than any serious structural overhaul.

And there have been few New Deal–style efforts at job creation or infrastructure investment. Yes, there was a $787 billion stimulus package passed in the early days of the Obama administration, but spending has been scattered and of dubious effectiveness. Obama's people bragged that they were trying to create private-sector jobs, not those evil public-sector ones like back in the 1930s. As a result, if you use their own numbers, they've "created or saved" fewer than a million jobs—against 8.5 million lost from December 2007 through December 2009—at a cost of $250,000 a job. The government could have created five times as many jobs had it hired people directly instead of relying on tax breaks and subsidies.

At the non-elite level, much of the population has been passive while the bankers got billions and the jobless got unemployment benefits (average weekly check in 2009: $305)—if they were lucky. Unlike in the 1930s, there's been no upsurge of union organizing, plant occupations, or solidarity with those facing foreclosure. Most of the noise has been coming from the far right—from, for example, the "Tea Baggers," nicely described by Ben McGrath in *The New Yorker* as a collection of "footloose Ron Paul supporters, goldbugs, evangelicals, Atlas Shruggers, militiamen, strict Constitutionalists, swine-flu skeptics, scattered 9/11 'truthers,' neo-'Birchers,' and, of course, 'birthers'—those who remained convinced that the President was a Muslim double agent born in Kenya." They appear to be a movement of middle managers, professionals, and retirees—not the 80 percent of the workforce classified as "nonsupervisory," the people who take orders on the job rather than giving them. (Those people, perched on the lower rungs of the economic ladder, now seem even more disenfranchised than ever.)

If this economic crisis has legs, which I think it does, then things may change. (Actually, if it is going to stick around, "crisis" is probably the wrong word to use to describe the new normal.) How long can people be expected to put up with enormously high levels of economic insecurity and crushing levels of debt? If people start recovering from the shocks of the last two years and want to begin to figure out what happened to them, then they could do no better than to pick up this fine book. It lays out not only what lawyerly types call the proximate causes of the crisis, such as the housing bubble and the mortgage mania, but the more enduring causes as well, such as deregulation and the assault on wages.

Though this crisis looks like it's of recent vintage, in fact its roots go back into the late 1970s. That's when elites decided that they'd had enough of insolent workers and rebellious colonies. At home, wages were slashed; abroad, entire continental economies were restructured into capital-friendly targets for foreign investment. Faced with sagging incomes, people borrowed to maintain their standards of living. And those restructured foreign economies became the new homes for the manufacturing plants that were shuttered in the Midwest. But we borrowed heavily to import all the stuff we used to make at home, and now U.S. households are massively in debt—and a lot of that money is owed to creditors abroad. Not only is it a brutal economic model, it no longer looks sustainable even on its own terms.

But Americans, elite and otherwise, haven't really figured this out yet. Instead, they imagine either a return to the boom of 2006 or the insular small-town all-white world of the 1840s. We'd be a lot better off if the people who picked up this book to figure out how we got here also took onboard the conclusion—the importance of tightening up financial regulation and of reinventing a culture of solidarity to replace the current survival-of-the-fittest model that's been imposed on us. That's a tall order, I know, but if we don't get started on the project now, we'll be back in crisis again—maybe before we even get out of this one.

UNDERSTANDING THE
CRASH

UNDERSTANDING THE
CRA$H

INTRODUCTION

HOW DID THIS HAPPEN ?????

IS THIS THE AMERICAN DREAM?

THIS FAMILY IS MOVING OUT.

THIS HOUSE

HAS BEEN

FORECLOSED.

WHOSE DREAM IS THIS?

BLOCK AFTER BLOCK OF BOARDED—UP BUILDINGS?

HOW DID THIS HAPPEN?

A MAN SHOWS UP FOR WORK AT THE SAME PLACE FOR YEARS.

THEN ONE DAY HE FINDS THAT THE PLANT HAS

CLOSED

AND HE IS BEING LET GO WITH NO SEVERANCE PAY, NO HEALTH CARE, NO PENSION.

WHEN FACTORIES CLOSE

STORES

CLOSE TOO.

WHOLE CITIES CHANGE.

A WOMAN GETS THE BEST HIGH-TECH EDUCATION

SO THAT SHE WILL QUALIFY FOR A HIGH-PAYING JOB.

AT FIRST SHE IS AMAZED!

THEN THE HIGH-TECH JOBS DISAPPEAR. SHE'S

LAID OFF!

NOW SHE IS UNEMPLOYED OR WORKING AT A JOB THAT PAYS LESS.

SHE IS LEFT WITH DEBTS SHE CAN'T PAY.

SHE TAKES A 2ND MORTGAGE.

AND THEN A 3RD.

INSTEAD OF BUYING NEW CARS AND FUR COATS, A COUPLE SAVE MONEY FOR THEIR RETIREMENT AND MEDICAL EXPENSES.

THEY GET THE ADVICE OF PROFESSIONALS ABOUT WHERE TO INVEST THEIR SAVINGS.

THEY ARE SURPRISED TO SEE HOW FAST THEIR MONEY GROWS.

THEN, IN A MOMENT,

25% OF THEIR SAVINGS DISAPPEAR.

LEHMAN BROTHERS WAS A WORLD-WIDE INVESTMENT GIANT.

LEHMAN BROTHERS

EMPLOYED 26,200 PEOPLE

AND HAD ASSETS WORTH $691.063 BILLION.

$10,000

$100

FOUNDED IN 1850,

LEHMAN WAS OVER 150 YEARS OLD.

BUT IN 2008 LEHMAN COLLAPSED IN A SINGLE DAY!

WHAT DOES THE BANKRUPTCY OF ONE OF THE BIGGEST FIRMS ON WALL STREET HAVE TO DO WITH THE BANKRUPTCY OF A HOME-OWNER IN CLEVELAND? HOW DOES BANKRUPTCY SPREAD WORLD-WIDE?

TODAY MANY OF US ARE LOOKING AT A CUT IN PAY OR EVEN THE LOSS OF A JOB. AND WE ARE TOLD THAT THIS HAS SOMETHING TO DO WITH THE BOARDED-UP HOUSE OR THE FAILED FINANCIAL FIRM. AND THIS SEEMS TO CONTRADICT EVERYTHING WE'VE BEEN TOLD ABOUT THE COUNTRY WE LIVE IN AND HOW WE SHOULD LIVE IN IT.

LEHMAN BROTHERS REST IN PEACE

WE WERE TOLD THAT THIS WAS THE RICHEST COUNTRY IN THE WORLD. THAT WE HAD STABLE INSTITU-TIONS AND A SYSTEM THAT "WORKED" FOR THOSE WHO TRIED.

WE WERE LED TO BELIEVE THAT IF WE WORKED HARD, WE COULD HAVE SECURE EMPLOYMENT.

THAT IF WE GOT AN EDUCATION, WE WOULD BE REWARDED WITH A BETTER POSITION.

THAT WE COULD EACH OWN A HOME AND IT WOULD INCREASE IN VALUE.

THAT IF WE SAVED OUR MONEY, WE COULD REST EASY KNOWING THAT WE WOULD BE COMFORTABLE IN OLD AGE.

THAT THE LIVES OF OUR CHILDREN WOULD BE BETTER THAN OUR LIVES, AS OUR LIVES HAD BEEN BETTER THAN THOSE OF OUR PARENTS.

THAT WE COULD EACH PURSUE OUR OWN DREAM AND BE WHATEVER WE WANTED TO BE.

SOME OF US CAME TO ASSUME THAT IF A PERSON WAS SUCCESSFUL, THIS WAS BECAUSE OF THEIR GOOD QUALITIES— INTELLIGENCE, INDUSTRIOUSNESS, EVEN HONESTY. WE WANTED TO BE AROUND THEM, TO BE LIKE THEM. WE SOUGHT THEIR ADVICE.

IF SOMEONE FAILED WE ASSUMED THAT THERE HAD TO BE SOMETHING WRONG WITH HIM.

BUT TODAY, EVERYONE KNOWS SOMEBODY WHO HAS LOST HIS HOME OR HIS JOB OR HIS SAVINGS.

AND WE'VE SEEN SOME VERY SUCCESSFUL PEOPLE BEING PROSECUTED FOR DEFRAUDING THEIR INVESTORS.

WE HAVE SEEN MAJOR BANKS GO BEGGING FOR A BAILOUT FROM OUR TAX DOLLARS.

HOW DID WE GET INTO THIS MESS AND HOW DO WE GET OUT OF IT? TO UNDERSTAND WHY THIS HAPPENED WE WILL HAVE TO TAKE A CLOSER LOOK AT HOW THE ECONOMY REALLY WORKS AND TO REEXAMINE SOME OF OUR BASIC ASSUMPTIONS ABOUT AMERICAN SOCIETY.

MRS. REDRICK'S LIVING ROOM:

THE REDRICKS PAID OFF THEIR 1st MORTGAGE

BUT HAD TO GO THROUGH 3 REFINANCES TO COVER REPAIRS.

BY 2005 SHE WAS LIVING ALONE ON A PENSION. SHE WAS HAVING A HARD TIME

MAKING HER MONTHLY MORTGAGE OF $600 PLUS TAX.

THAT'S WHEN SHE GOT A CALL

FROM A HANDSOME YOUNG MAN NAMED GEORGE.

MRS. REDRICK

I CAN MAKE YOUR MONTHLY PAYMENTS LOWER.

SHE WENT TO GEORGE'S OFFICE, WHERE HE CONVINCED MRS. REDRICK

TO SIGN UP FOR A NEW MORTGAGE THROUGH HIM.

SHE SIGNED A FORM SHE NEVER READ, A FORM FILLED OUT BY GEORGE, FULL OF MISINFORMATION.

IT SAID SHE WAS WHITE, LIVED NEAR SHAKER HEIGHTS, ALL TO MAKE HER LOOK LIKE A BETTER CREDIT RISK.

GEORGE TOLD HER SHE COULD STOP PAYING HER MONTHLY MORTGAGE, THAT IT ALL WOULD BE TAKEN CARE OF WHEN THE DEAL "CLOSED."

FOR THE NEXT 3 MONTHS SHE DIDN'T PAY HER MORTGAGE. HER DEBTS BUILT UP AS SHE WAITED FOR THE DEAL TO "CLOSE."

SUDDENLY GEORGE BROUGHT HER A NEW CONTRACT. SAID SHE HAD TO SIGN IT TO CLOSE THE DEAL AND PAY HER DEBT.

HER MONTHLY MORTGAGE WENT UP TO $700. HOMEOWNERS INSURANCE WENT UP FROM $680 TO $4,000! IT WAS MORE THAN SHE COULD PAY.

SHE WOULD PAY PART OF IT, HOPING TO PAY THE REST LATER. BUT THE SERVICER WOULD NOT ACCEPT PARTIAL PAYMENT. THE SERVICER PREFERRED TO FORECLOSE HER HOME.

I NEVER HEARD ANYTHING LIKE THIS! IF I WASN'T TRYIN' T' PAY IT, THAT'D BE DIFFERENT! IF I HADN'T BEEN PAYIN' FOR ALL THOSE YEARS I WOULDN'T A' BEEN IN THAT HOUSE!

SO I SAID, "LET ME GET SOME HELP."

MRS. REDRICK GOT THE HELP OF ED, A LAWYER WITH A NONPROFIT LEGAL CLINIC.

ED WENT TO COURT ON HER BEHALF.

THE COURT CASE TOOK 2 YEARS, DURING WHICH TIME MRS. REDRICK MADE PAYMENTS INTO AN ESCROW ACCOUNT.

AS HER CASE DRAGGED ON, MANY HOUSES IN MRS. REDRICK'S NEIGHBORHOOD WENT INTO FORCLOSURE. MRS. REDRICK WAS SOON SURROUNDED BY ABANDONED HOMES. THE PRICE OF A HOME IN THE AREA WENT DOWN.

WHEN ONE PERSON LOSES THEIR HOME IT'S TRAGIC. WHAT HAPPENS TO A COMMUNITY WHEN MANY HOUSES ARE FORECLOSED?

RIGHT THROUGH THE HEART OF THE RUST BELT CITY OF CLEVELAND

FLOWS A WATERFALL.

ORIGINALLY A DUMP SITE FOR A TRUCKING COMPANY, THIS PARK WAS CLEANED UP BY A COMMUNITY ORGANIZATION.

THE NEIGHBORHOOD
(THE FREE TRADE ZONE)

THE PARK SITS BETWEEN TWO WORKING-CLASS COMMUNITIES, SLAVIC VILLAGE AND UNION-MILES.

EVEN BEFORE THE CURRENT CRISIS, UNION-MILES HAD ALWAYS BEEN UNDERSERVED.

THERE IS NO BANK, NO DRUG STORE, ONLY ONE GROCERY.

THERE IS NO POLICE STATION AND NO FIRE DEPARTMENT. FIRE TRUCKS COME FROM THE FIREHOUSE IN SLAVIC VILLAGE 10 MINUTES AWAY.

TEN MINUTES IS A LONG TIME IF YOUR HOUSE IS BURNING.

JOHN ADAMS HIGH WAS DEMOLISHED IN 1995 AND DID NOT REOPEN UNTIL 2002. UNION-MILES WENT 7 YEARS WITHOUT A HIGH SCHOOL.

IN SPITE OF GOVERNMENT NEGLECT, MANY IN UNION-MILES TAKE PRIDE IN THEIR COMMUNITY AND THEIR HOMES.

BUT NOW THEY ARE SURROUNDED BY EMPTY HOUSES.

SOME BECAME EMPTY BECAUSE OWNERS

DIED WITHOUT LEAVING A WILL...

OTHERS WERE FORECLOSED BECAUSE OWNERS WERE

SWINDLED BY LOAN SHARKS!

WHEN LANDLORDS GO INTO FORCLOSURE THEY OFTEN FAIL TO TELL TENANTS, WHO KEEP PAYING RENT TILL THE SHERIFF EVICTS THEM.

IF FOLKS MOVE OUT IN THE MORNING...

BY NIGHT-FALL, THE METAL-STRIPPING OPERATION IS STEALING COPPER PIPES.

THE METAL IS SOLD TO SCRAP YARDS. THERE IS A BIG DEMAND FOR THIS METAL IN FOREIGN COUNTRIES.

METAL STRIPPERS HAVE BECOME SO BOLD THAT THEY STEAL METAL OFF BUILDINGS THAT AREN'T EMPTY. THE SCHOOL HAS LOST BOTH DRAIN PIPES AND FENCES.

THE "WOLVES" TAKE OVER. DRUG DEALERS START WORKING OUT OF THE EMPTY HOUSES.

STREET CLUBS STOP MEETING BECAUSE THEY HAVE BEEN THREATENED. POLICE DO NOT INTERFERE.

WHOLE BLOCKS FALL UNDER CONTROL OF THE CRIMINAL ENTERPRISE.

UNION-MILES HAS BECOME A FREE TRADE ZONE WHERE DRUG DEALERS AND PREDATORY LENDERS CAN MAKE MONEY AS THEY PLEASE.

MARK WISEMAN, DIRECTOR OF THE FORECLOSURE PREVENTION PROGRAM

CUYAHOGA COUNTY HAS LOST MORE PEOPLE THAN ANY COUNTY NOT HIT BY HURRICANE KATRINA. WHAT WE'RE LOOKING AT IS THE DE-URBANIZATION OF CLEVELAND.

YES, THE WATER-FALL IS BEAUTIFUL. BUT WHO WILL BE THERE TO SEE IT?

CITIES LIKE CLEVELAND HAVE IT BAD. BUT THE SUN BELT IS DIFFERENT. OR IS IT?

MIAMI, FLORIDA'S MOST IMPORTANT PRODUCT IS MIAMI, FLORIDA.

TOURISTS COME FOR THE BEACHES; SENIORS RETIRE IN WARM WEATHER.

MIAMI

A TYPICAL MIAMI OFFICE BUILDING MAY HOUSE:

A MORTGAGE BROKER
LANDSCAPE ARCHITECT
CONTRACT-OR
INSUR-ANCE AGENT

REAL ESTATE DEVELOPMENT IS A BIG BUSINESS HERE, PROVIDING MANY JOBS.

MORE SUB-DIVISIONS.

MORE STRIP MALLS.

HERE THE ENGINE OF GROWTH IS GROWTH. BUT WHAT IF GROWTH STOPS?

BOOMBUST

MIAMI'S POST-WWII BOOM WAS FUELED BY UNION PENSION PLANS. FROM YEARS OF STRUGGLE UNIONS HAD ATTAINED A BETTER STANDARD OF LIVING FOR WORKERS, INCLUDING PENSIONS.

AS A WORKER, YOU WOULD GET A "DEFINED BENEFIT PLAN." UNDER THE MOST COMMON VERSION, A "FINAL AVERAGE PAY PLAN" BASED YOUR PENSION ON THE AVERAGE SALARY OF THE LAST FEW YEARS YOU WORKED. AND YOU WOULD RECEIVE THAT PENSION EVERY MONTH, FROM THE DAY YOU RETIRED, FOR THE REST OF YOUR LIFE.

IT ALSO HELPED THAT THERE WAS A HEALTHY HOUSING MARKET IN PLACES LIKE THE MIDWEST SO RETIREES COULD SELL THEIR HOMES AND MOVE TO CONDOMINIUMS IN MIAMI.

AT ONE POINT, IT WAS CLAIMED, A THOUSAND NEW RESIDENTS A DAY MOVED TO FLORIDA.

FOR YEARS CONSTRUCTION OF NEW UNITS DIDN'T KEEP PACE WITH NEW ARRIVALS.

THEY WERE BUILDING ABOUT ONE UNIT FOR EVERY 19 NEW PEOPLE.

BUT BETWEEN 2000-2007 THE PACE OF CONSTRUCTION INCREASED TO 1 UNIT FOR EVERY 2 ARRIVALS.

LOANS FOR NEW CONSTRUCTION HAD BECOME MORE AVAILABLE BECAUSE ALAN GREENSPAN, HEAD OF THE FEDERAL RESERVE, HAD CUT THE INTEREST RATE BANKS PAY WHEN THEY BORROW MONEY FROM THE FED DOWN TO 1%.

BANKS CAN CHARGE A HIGHER INTEREST RATE WHEN THEY LOAN OUT THAT MONEY TO THE PUBLIC, SO THE DIFFERENCE BETWEEN THESE TWO INTEREST RATES AFFECTS THEIR PROFIT MARGIN.

GREENSPAN HAD MADE IT MORE PROFITABLE FOR BANKS TO LEND MONEY.

IT ALSO BECAME MORE PROFITABLE FOR BANKS TO LEND MONEY

BECAUSE REGULATIONS ON BANKING HAD BEEN RELAXED.

AS MORTGAGES BECAME EASIER TO OBTAIN, CONSTRUCTION BEGAN TO SPEED UP.

THE PRICE OF MIAMI HOUSING ALSO ROSE. IT WAS EVEN ON THE NEWS.

I BOUGHT THIS HOUSE FOR $200,000 AND 6 MONTHS LATER I SOLD IT FOR $250,000!

SUCH TALES LED MANY MIDDLE CLASS PEOPLE TO GET INVOLVED IN THE "FLIPPING" GAME.

"FLIPPING" IS BUYING A HOUSE, NOT TO LIVE IN IT,

RATHER, TO TURN AROUND AND SELL IT

AT A PROFIT.

RISING HOME PRICES PRESENTED TEMPTATION. LET'S SAY YOU FOUND OUT THAT YOUR HOUSE HAD GONE UP IN VALUE BY $125,000.

IN THAT CASE, A BANK MIGHT OFFER TO MAKE YOU A LOAN.

YOU COULD TAKE OUT A 2ND MORTGAGE AGAINST YOUR HOME

AND USE THAT MONEY TO BUY A 2ND HOUSE TO PLAY THE FLIPPING GAME.

YOU WOULD BE GAMBLING WITH THE VERY HOUSE YOU LIVED IN.

BUT NEWSPAPERS AND BUSINESS SHOWS WOULD ASSURE YOU THAT HOUSE PRICES COULD NEVER GO DOWN.

MO-Money

SOME PEOPLE ALSO TOOK OUT LOANS AGAINST THEIR HOMES TO INVEST THAT MONEY IN STARTING UP...

ONE DOLLAR

A SMALL BUSINESS.

MY LIL' SHOP

GEORGE W. BUSH CALLED IT THE "OWNERSHIP SOCIETY,"

IN WHICH EVERYONE CAN BE A CAPITALIST,

A TINY TRUMP, A MINI-J.P. MORGAN, A STEVE JOBS JR.

A SUCKER.

IN AUGUST 2007, MIAMI'S HOUSING MARKET COLLAPSED.

ONE OF THE CAUSES OF THE MIAMI HOUSING MARKET COLLAPSE WAS THAT BACK IN THE 1980S, EMPLOYERS HAD REPLACED THE "DEFINED BENEFIT PLAN," WHICH UNIONS HAD FOUGHT FOR, WITH THE "DEFINED CONTRIBUTION PLAN," OR 401(K). UNDER THE 401(K) THERE WAS NO GUARANTEED PENSION.

WORKERS INVESTED PART OF THEIR PAYCHECKS INTO RETIREMENT ACCOUNTS. IF THE EMPLOYER PUT OUT ANYTHING AT ALL IT WAS OFTEN IN THE FORM OF COMPANY STOCK. MANY WORKERS SAW THE VALUE OF THEIR 401(K)s PLUMMET IN 2001-2002 WHEN THE STOCK OF COMPANIES LIKE ENRON BECAME WORTHLESS. PEOPLE WHO'D PLANNED TO RETIRE HAD TO KEEP WORKING. SOME RETIREES EVEN WENT BACK TO WORK.

WHEN THE PRICE OF HOUSES DROPPED IN CITIES LIKE DETROIT OR CLEVELAND A FEW YEARS LATER, RETIREES COULD NO LONGER SELL THEIR HOMES AND MOVE TO MIAMI.

ANOTHER REASON FOR THE COLLAPSE
WAS THAT REAL ESTATE IN PLACES
LIKE MIAMI WAS SIMPLY TOO
EXPENSIVE. A SPECULATIVE
BOOM HAD PUSHED HOUSE
PRICES UP SO HIGH
THAT FEW FOLKS
COULD AFFORD
TO BUY.

POPULATION INCREASE VS. CONDO CONSTRUCTION
OVER TEN YEARS

350,000 — 60,000
300,000 — 50,000
250,000 — 40,000
200,000 — 30,000
150,000 — 20,000
100,000
50,000 — 10,000
0 — 0

CONDO UNITS BUILT

1970-79   1980-89   1990-99   2...

LOOKING AT THOSE FIGURES AGAIN: WHILE THE RATE OF CONSTRUCTION HAD GONE UP, THE ACTUAL NUMBER OF PEOPLE MOVING TO MIAMI HAD GONE DOWN. FROM 300,000 IN THE '90s TO ABOUT 116,000 IN THE CURRENT DECADE.

WITHOUT A STEADY STREAM OF NEW RETIREES, THE GROWTH MACHINE BEGINS TO RUN IN REVERSE.

37

THE WOMAN WHO INTENDED TO "FLIP" A HOUSE NOW CAN'T FIND A BUYER. CAN'T PAY HER MORTGAGE. MUST DEFAULT. THE WOMAN WITH 2 HOUSES IS NOW HOMELESS.

REAL-ESTATE-RELATED FIRMS GO UNDER OR LAY OFF WORKERS. THERE IS MASSIVE UNEMPLOYMENT!

CLOSED CLOSED CLOSED CLOSED CLO

MALLS ARE EMPTY. STORES CLOSE.

MY LIL' SHO

BIG REAL ESTATE DEVELOPERS ARE STARTING TO SAY "DON'T GIVE ME ANYTHING WITH SAND IN IT." THEY DON'T WANT TO PUT MONEY INTO CALIFORNIA, ARIZONA, NEVADA, OR FLORIDA.

FLORIDA

THE TRADITIONAL RETIREMENT HAVENS HAVE BEEN REDLINED.

THE ICON, AN 1,800-UNIT LUXURY CONDO HAS SOLD ONLY 31 UNITS.

IN DADE COUNTY, RECENTLY BUILT SUBDIVISIONS SIT EMPTY.

THE SWIMMING POOLS TURN GREEN. YARDS FILL UP WITH SNAKES.

THE "SUN BELT"

LOOKS A LOT LIKE THE "RUST BELT." THERE ARE SHARKS IN THOSE WATERS.

EVEN BEFORE THE HOUSING MARKET CRASHED, THERE WAS ALWAYS A SINISTER SIDE TO MIAMI'S REAL ESTATE BOOM.

MORE AND MORE OF THE EVERGLADES HAD TO BE BULLDOZED TO BUILD NEW SUBDIVISIONS.

IF THE OWNERSHIP SOCIETY TRASHED THE EVERGLADES, IT ALSO HURT MIAMI'S POOR. A HOT HOUSING MARKET IS GOOD FOR SOME PEOPLE AND BAD FOR OTHERS. IF YOU ARE A PROPERTY OWNER OR A DEVELOPER, WHAT YOU OWN GOES UP IN VALUE, BUT IF YOU ARE A POOR PERSON LOOKING TO BUY YOUR FIRST HOME, RISING PRICES MIGHT MAKE YOUR DREAM IMPOSSIBLE. IF YOU ARE A RENTER, YOUR LANDLORD MIGHT EVICT YOU SO HE CAN GET A HIGHER PRICE FROM SOME- ONE ELSE. IN OTHER WORDS, GENTRIFICATION.

THE CRUEL BOOM

YOU WOULD THINK THAT THE MIAMI HOUSING AUTHORITY WOULD BE DOING SOMETHING TO HELP THE POOR SURVIVE THE HOUSING SHORTAGE. NOT!

M.H.A.

INSTEAD, IN 1999, THEY BEGAN TO DEMOLISH THE SCOTT CARVER HOUSING PROJECTS.

THEY SAID THEY WAS GONNA TEAR THE PLACES DOWN, REMODEL 'EM, IN ORDER FOR PEOPLE TO COME BACK. THEY ALSO SAID IF YOUR CREDIT WAS GOOD, YOU COULD GET A HOUSE.

MS. CORA →

NOT!

INSTEAD, CORA WOULD BE PUSHED FROM ONE PLACE TO ANOTHER UNTIL SHE WOUND UP SLEEPING IN HER TRUCK.

MEANWHILE, DEVELOPERS AND PUBLIC OFFICIALS WERE POCKETING THE MONEY THAT HAD BEEN ALLOCATED

H.U.D.

FOR REBUILDING THE PROJECTS.

EVENTUALLY SOME OF THESE VILLAINS WERE CAUGHT AND PROSECUTED.

BUT THE PROJECTS WERE NOT REBUILT.

DESTROYING PUBLIC HOUSING RAISED MIAMI REAL ESTATE VALUES.

CORA JOINED WITH THE MIAMI WORKERS CENTER AND OTHER DISPLACED PROJECT TENANTS TO FIGHT FOR A HOME. THEIR FIRST PROBLEM WAS THAT SCOTT CARVER FOLKS HAD BEEN DISPERSED ALL OVER THE CITY. HOW TO FIND THEM AND ORGANIZE THEM?

ACTIVISTS SET UP A WALL WITH THE NAMES OF FORMER RESIDENTS NEAR THE SITE OF THE DEMOLISHED PROJECTS. PEOPLE WHO SAW THEIR NAMES WERE RECRUITED INTO THE CAMPAIGN.

SOON HUNDREDS OF SCOTT CARVER RESIDENTS WERE MARCH-ING IN THE STREET TO DEMAND HOUSING.

THE RESULT WAS THAT CORA AND OTHERS WERE PLACED IN PUBLIC HOUSING.

H.U.D.

ALTHOUGH SCOTT CARVER WAS NEVER REBUILT.

AND H.U.D. HAS PLACED CORA IN A HOME-OWNERSHIP PROGRAM, WHERE THEY AGAIN TELL HER

THAT SHE CAN GET A HOUSE IF SHE JUST "IMPROVES HER CREDIT RATING!"

IN MIAMI'S HOT HOUSING MARKET A CONSTELLATION OF ANTI-GENTRIFICATION GROUPS HAVE FORMED. FOR THEM, THE HOUSING CRASH IS NOT SUCH A BAD THING.

LIFFT

TAKE BACK THE LAND

POWER U

WORKERS CENTER

ONE OF THE NATIONAL POSITIONS AROUND THE DESTRUCTION OF PUBLIC HOUSING HAS BEEN THAT "CONCENTRATED POVERTY IS DANGEROUS." THEY SAY TOO MANY POOR PEOPLE TOGETHER IS BAD. WE FEEL LIKE YOU COULD FLIP THAT. 'CAUSE RIGHT NOW THE CONCENTRATED WEALTH IN THIS AREA IS NOT HELPFUL. HALF OF IT'S EMPTY CONDO HIGH-RISES, SO WE COULD MOVE PEOPLE INTO THOSE IF H.U.D. WANTS TO FULFILL THEIR 71,000-PERSON WAITING LIST FOR PUBLIC HOUSING. IT COULD BE A COMPLETE FLIP IN THE SCRIPT!

DENISE PERRY OF POWER U.

IF HOMEOWNERSHIP IS THE AMERICAN DREAM, HOW DID HOME MORTGAGES BECOME SUCH A NIGHTMARE?

A HOME OF ONE'S OWN USED TO BE ONE OF THE LEAST RISKY INVESTMENTS A PERSON COULD MAKE.

BUT UNLESS YOU WERE RICH, YOU COULD NOT GET A HOUSE WITH-OUT A MORTGAGE.

POOR PEOPLE AND PEOPLE OF COLOR

COUNTRY BANK

WHEN THE POOR DID GET LOANS, THEY WERE OFTEN RISKY "SUBPRIME" MORTGAGES WHICH USUALLY CHARGED A HIGHER INTEREST RATE. AND SUBPRIME MORTGAGES USED TO BE RARE.

SUBPRIME

IN THE POST-WWII ERA THERE WAS A PRACTICE OF DENYING LOANS TO LOW-INCOME NEIGHBORHOODS.

IT WAS CALLED "REDLINING."

IN THE '60S & '70S FOLKS PROTESTED REDLINING.

COUNTRY BANK

SO UNCLE SAM MADE BANKS REVEAL THEIR LENDING PRACTICES.

BANKS WERE MADE TO OPEN BRANCHES IN "BLIGHTED" AREAS AND MAKE LOANS THERE.

BUT REDLINING IS WIDELY BELIEVED TO CONTINUE.

48

BUT FOR THE MIDDLE CLASS, MORTGAGES USED TO BE PRETTY SIMPLE. THE STANDARD MORTGAGE WAS KNOWN AS A "30-YEAR FIXED."

IT REQUIRED STEADY MONTHLY PAYMENTS FROM THE BUYER TO BE COMPLETED, INCLUDING INTEREST, IN 30 YEARS.

BUT, STARTING IN THE 1970'S, BANKS BEGAN TO EXPERIMENT WITH COMPLEX NEW TYPES OF MORTGAGES. THESE BIZARRE "PRODUCTS" WERE MORE PROFITABLE TO BANKS AND OFTEN APPEARED TO CONSUMERS TO BE MORE AFFORDABLE. BUT IN THE LONG RUN, THESE NEW MORTGAGES WOULD PROVE TO BE RISKY FOR BOTH BANKS AND BORROWERS.

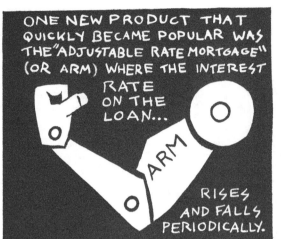
ONE NEW PRODUCT THAT QUICKLY BECAME POPULAR WAS THE "ADJUSTABLE RATE MORTGAGE" (OR ARM) WHERE THE INTEREST RATE ON THE LOAN... RISES AND FALLS PERIODICALLY.

ARM'S CAN START OUT MUCH CHEAPER THAN FIXED-RATE MORTGAGES. SO, FOR THE FIRST FEW YEARS, THE INTEREST RATE ON AN ARM MIGHT SEEM LOW.

BUT AFTER A FEW YEARS, THE RATE MIGHT INCREASE.

CHANGES IN RATES ON ARM'S ARE TIED TO CHANGES IN SOME ECONOMIC INDICATORS. THE MOST COMMONLY USED INDICATORS ARE INTEREST RATES ON TREASURY BONDS.

MANY HOME-OWNERS DID NOT UNDERSTAND THESE INDICATORS.

THE LOWER INITIAL PAYMENTS MADE IT POSSIBLE TO APPROVE MANY PEOPLE FOR MORTGAGES WHO WOULDN'T HAVE QUALIFIED FOR THE OLD "30-YEAR FIXED" LOANS.

MANY SUBPRIME MORTGAGES WERE ARM'S. THE PEOPLE WITH THE LEAST ABILITY TO PAY WERE TAKING THE HIGHEST RISK.

THESE FOLKS WERE BETTING THAT THEIR INCOMES WOULD INCREASE IN A FEW YEARS SO THEY COULD PAY THE HIGHER RATES. THEY WERE ALSO GAMBLING THAT THEIR HOMES WOULD GO UP IN VALUE. IF THIS HAPPENED, BANKS WOULD BE HAPPY TO LET THEM BORROW AGAINST THAT VALUE BY TAKING OUT HOME EQUITY LOANS. THEY COULD TAKE OUT A 2ND MORTGAGE TO PAY OFF THE 1ST.

IT'S UNDERSTANDABLE WHY A PERSON IN NEED OF A HOME WOULD TAKE A RISK. BUT WHY WOULD A BANK GAMBLE IN THIS WAY?

BECAUSE BANKS WEREN'T KEEPING THOSE LOANS ON THEIR BOOKS. BANKS THAT ORIGINATED MORTGAGES WERE SELLING THOSE MORTGAGES TO LARGER BANKS. GOVERNMENT DEREGULATION HAD MADE THIS EASY TO DO.

ORIGINATING BANK

PURCHASING BANK

LOANS

THE PURCHASING BANK TURNED THE MORTGAGES INTO "MORTGAGE-BACKED SECURITIES" OR MBS's.

BUT PURCHASING BANKS DIDN'T KEEP THE MBS's ON THEIR BOOKS FOR LONG EITHER. THEY SOLD THEM TO BIG INSTITUTIONAL INVESTORS — PENSION FUNDS, MUTUAL FUNDS, BIG PRIVATE INVESTORS, AND INSURANCE COMPANIES.

THE INVESTORS WERE TAKING A RISK, BUT AT THE TIME IT LOOKED LIKE A VERY PROFITABLE RISK BECAUSE INVESTORS WHO OWNED MORTGAGE-BACKED SECURITIES

RECEIVED A CUT OUT OF THOUSANDS OF PEOPLE'S MONTHLY MORTGAGE PAYMENTS. THAT'S A LOT OF MONEY!

SALE

SO, NATURALLY, DEMAND FOR MBS'S GOT HUGE. SO WALL STREET GOT BUSY, CREATING NEW TYPES OF MBS'S. THE STRUCTURES GREW MORE ELABORATE AND MORE CONFUSING.

THE MOST POPULAR WERE COLLATERALIZED MORTGAGE OBLIGATIONS, CMO'S, THAT COULD BE CUT INTO SECTIONS AND RESOLD,

AND CDO'S, WHICH COMBINED MORTGAGES WITH OTHER TYPES OF DEBT. CREDIT CARDS, AUTO LOANS. BY COMBINING RISKY DEBT WITH MORE CREDIT-WORTHY LOANS CDO'S WERE SUPPOSED TO BE SAFER.

BUT THIS ALSO MADE IT HARD FOR INVESTORS TO KNOW WHAT THEY WERE BUYING.

SO WHY DID INVESTORS BUY SUCH RISKY STUFF? 3 REASONS:

#1 BECAUSE WALL STREET FIRMS THAT PACKAGED MBS'S HAD STAFFS OF "EXPERTS" WHO PRESENTED EQUATIONS TO PROVE THE SAFETY OF THEIR PRODUCTS.

#2 RATING AGENCIES ALSO SAID IT WAS SAFE. BUT THESE AGENCIES WERE PAID BY THE BANKS, NOT THE INVESTORS.

#3 THEY THOUGHT THEY WERE INSURED. ONE OF WALL STREET'S HOTTEST ITEMS WAS THE

A BIG INVESTOR THAT OWNED A LOT OF CDO'S COULD GO TO A BANK AND TAKE OUT A CREDIT DEFAULT SWAP AGAINST THE CDO'S, WHICH MEANT THE BANK WOULD PAY THE INVESTOR IF THE CDO'S WENT DOWN IN VALUE DUE TO FORECLOSURES. THIS SORT OF DEAL WAS REFERRED TO AS A "DERIVATIVE."

BUT IT WAS ALSO POSSIBLE TO TAKE OUT A CREDIT DEFAULT SWAP AGAINST A CDO THAT YOU DIDN'T OWN,

IN EFFECT MAKING A BET THAT FOLKS WOULD LOSE THEIR HOMES. CREDIT DEFAULT SWAPS TURNED INVESTING INTO CASINO GAMBLING.

AS IT TURNED OUT, CREDIT DEFAULT SWAPS WERE NEITHER A GOOD BET NOR A REAL INSURANCE POLICY. THE SELLER OF A CREDIT DEFAULT SWAP WAS NOT REQUIRED TO BACK IT UP WITH ANY RESERVES OF CASH. SO IF A LOT OF HOMES WERE FORECLOSED AND A LOT OF MORTGAGE-BACKED SECURITIES WENT BAD, THERE WOULD BE NO MONEY TO PAY THE BUYER.

BUT GREED IS BLIND. BIG BANKS BEGAN TO BELIEVE THEIR OWN HYPE. WALL STREET FIRMS, LIKE LEHMAN BROTHERS AND MERRILL LYNCH, WEREN'T JUST SELLING CMO'S AND CDO'S TO THEIR INVESTORS ANY MORE. WANTING A PIECE OF THE ACTION, THEY WERE BUYING THEM AND HOLDING THEM ON THEIR BOOKS.

AND THIS, IN THE END, WOULD LEAD TO THEIR DOWNFALL.

AS DEBT BECAME A PRODUCT THAT BANKS COULD BUY, SELL, AND SPECULATE ON, THEY RELAXED THEIR STANDARDS FOR WHOM THEY GAVE LOANS TO. THE MORE A PERSON OWED, THE MORE OF THIS VALUABLE DEBT THERE WAS TO SELL. IF THEY TOOK OUT A 2ND OR 3RD MORTGAGE, EVEN BETTER. AS LONG AS THE DEBTOR KEPT MAKING PAY-MENTS.

THE MORTGAGE MARKET HAD BECOME A CASINO.

LOCAL BANKS WERE THE DEALERS. WALL STREET WAS THE HOUSE.

THE GAMBLERS WERE THE AMERICAN MIDDLE CLASS.

IN LATE 2006, SOME BIG BANKS BECAME WORRIED AND STOPPED BUYING SOME OF THE RISKIER MORTGAGES.

THE CASINO COLLAPSED, LEAVING ORDINARY FOLKS STARING AT THEIR LOSSES.

BEFORE 1933, BANKS WERE FREE TO PERFORM MANY FUNCTIONS AT THE SAME TIME. A BANK WHERE YOU PUT YOUR SAVINGS AND TOOK OUT YOUR MORTGAGE COULD ALSO BUY AND SELL STOCKS, BONDS, AND SECURITIES, IN EFFECT PLAYING THE MARKET WITH YOUR MONEY. THEY COULD EVEN SELL INSURANCE.

FOR EXAMPLE, J.P. MORGAN TRUST COULD MAKE MONEY MANY WAYS:

THERE WAS A CONFLICT OF INTEREST, BECAUSE, OFTEN, THE BANK WOULD PERSUADE INVESTORS WHO WERE ITS CLIENTS TO BUY STOCKS AND BONDS ISSUED BY COMPANIES THAT IT HAD LENT MONEY TO. BANKS BECAME TOO BIG, TOO POWERFUL, TOOK ON TOO MUCH RISK. THEY BECAME SO BIG THAT THEIR BANKRUPTCY MIGHT TAKE OUT THE WHOLE ECONOMY. THEY WERE "TOO BIG TO FAIL."

SAVINGS ACCOUNTS

LOANS

OWNING RAILROADS

LENDING MONEY TO GOVERNMENTS

STEEL MILLS

MANAGING MONEY FOR THE RICH

POWER PLANTS

REINVENTING THE OCTOPUS

IN 1929 THE STOCK MARKET CRASHED, LEADING TO THE GREAT DEPRESSION. IN RESPONSE, AMERICANS SENT FRANKLIN DELANO ROOSEVELT TO THE WHITE HOUSE. HE PROMISED A "NEW DEAL" FOR THE U.S. ECONOMY. SHORTLY AFTERWARD, FACED WITH A RUN ON THE BANKS, ROOSEVELT TEMPORARILY CLOSED THEM. AFTER THEY REOPENED, THE GOVERNMENT CREATED A NEW REGULATORY FRAMEWORK FOR BANKS TO HEAD OFF FUTURE CRISES. THE MOST IMPORTANT PIECE OF LEGISLATION WAS GLASS-STEAGALL, PROPERLY NAMED THE "BANKING ACT OF 1933"

UNDER GLASS-STEAGALL, THE FINANCIAL SERVICES BUSINESS WAS SPLIT UP INTO THREE AREAS. A BANK WHICH OPERATED IN ONE AREA HAD TO STAY OUT OF THE OTHER TWO.

FDR WANTED UNCLE SAM TO ...REGULATE

THE BANKS AND BIG BUSINESS. TO PROTECT THE PUBLIC. TO PROTECT BANKS FROM THEIR OWN MISTAKES.

BUT HE DIDN'T WANT TO DISCOURAGE BANKS FROM LENDING TO FIRST—TIME HOME BUYERS. "FANNIE MAE" (THE FEDERAL NATIONAL MORTGAGE ASSISTANCE CORPORATION) WAS SET UP AS A GOVERNMENT—OWNED COMPANY TO BUY MORTGAGES FROM BANKS SO THAT BANKS COULD ISSUE MORE MORTGAGES. IN THE 1960s, WASHINGTON PRIVATIZED FANNIE MAE AND SET UP ANOTHER PRIVATE COMPANY, "FREDDIE MAC," TO COMPETE WITH FANNIE MAE.

FDR's IDEAS WORKED!

THE '50s AND '60s ARE REMEMBERED AS DECADES OF PROSPERITY, SO ROOSEVELT'S REFORMS WERE POPULAR.

BUT SOME DISAGREED. RICH BUSINESSMEN WANTED TO DEREGULATE SO THEY COULD MAKE MORE MONEY. THEY HAD THEIR ADVOCATES.

WRITERS SUCH AS AYN RAND, POLITICIANS SUCH AS REAGAN AND GOLDWATER, ECONOMISTS SUCH AS MILTON FRIEDMAN.

THEY ALSO SET UP "THINK TANKS" LIKE THE HERITAGE FOUNDATION TO PROMOTE THEIR VIEWS.

THEIR PUBLIC RELATIONS CAMPAIGN WORKED. DEREGULATION BECAME THE HOTTEST TREND IN GOVERNMENT.

FOR 30 YEARS, UNDER DEMOCRATIC AS WELL AS REPUBLICAN ADMINISTRATIONS, GOVERNMENT SUPERVISION WAS RELAXED OR ELIMINATED IN ONE INDUSTRY AFTER ANOTHER: RAILROADS, ELECTRIC POWER, TV, NEWSPAPERS, AIRLINES.

NEW!

IMPROVED!

DEREGULATED!

A STOCK MARKET SLUMP IN THE EARLY 1970s, FOLLOWED BY A SEVERE RECESSION, REDUCED THE NUMBER OF PEOPLE WHO WANTED TO BUY STOCK AT BROKERAGE HOUSES. TO HELP THE HOUSES, UNCLE SAM ABOLISHED REGULATIONS ON THE COMMISSIONS BROKERAGE HOUSES CHARGE. HE FIGURED THAT IF THEY WERE FREE TO CHARGE LOWER RATES, THEIR BUSINESS WOULD COME BACK.

IT DID. THE VOLUME OF TRADING WENT WAY UP, BUT WALL STREET BECAME A DIFFERENT PLACE.

STOCKS AND BONDS TRADED MORE FREQUENTLY. THE BROKERAGE BUSINESS BECAME MORE COMPLEX. SO INVESTMENT BANKS EXPANDED AND BOUGHT NEW TECHNOLOGY TO KEEP TRACK OF IT ALL.

ONLY THE LARGER FIRMS COULD AFFORD TO EXPAND SO MUCH. THEY BOUGHT OUT THEIR COMPETITORS. A WAVE OF MERGERS CONCENTRATED INVESTMENT BANKING IN MONSTER FIRMS LIKE:

MERRILL LYNCH, GOLDMAN SACHS AND MORGAN STANLEY.

THEIR TRADING DESKS STARTED TAKING BIGGER RISKS. SOME—TIMES THEY REAPED HUGE PROFITS. SOMETIMES THEY TOOK LOSSES. THEY BEGAN TO SELL NEW PRODUCTS WITH WEIRD NAMES.

IN THE EARLY 1970s FANNIE AND FREDDIE BEGAN TO SELL MBS's TO PRIVATE INVESTORS.

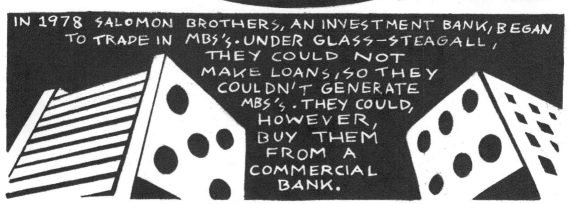

IN 1978 SALOMON BROTHERS, AN INVESTMENT BANK, BEGAN TO TRADE IN MBS's. UNDER GLASS—STEAGALL, THEY COULD NOT MAKE LOANS, SO THEY COULDN'T GENERATE MBS's. THEY COULD, HOWEVER, BUY THEM FROM A COMMERCIAL BANK.

MEANWHILE, A VICIOUS BOOM-AND-BUST CYCLE BEGAN. SOME OF THESE CRASHES WERE THE RESULT OF INTERNATIONAL, ECONOMIC, OR POLITICAL TENSIONS. BUT OTHERS WERE CAUSED DIRECTLY BY DEREGULATION.

1979 OIL PRICE SHOCK

1982 LATIN AMERICAN DEBT CRISIS

1987 STOCK MARKET CRASH

1989 SAVINGS AND LOAN COLLAPSE

1994 MEXICAN DEBT CRISIS

1997-8 ASIAN-RUSSIAN DEBT CRISIS

2000 DOT COM

EACH TIME THERE WAS A CRASH, WALL STREET PERSUADED CONGRESS THAT THE KEY TO RECOVERY WAS MORE DEREGULATION.

AND SO FDR'S LEGACY WAS TAKEN APART, PIECE BY PIECE, YEAR BY YEAR.

1982 THE ALTERNATIVE MORTGAGE TRANSACTIONS PARITY ACT EASED RESTRICTIONS ON ARM'S.

ARM

1986 THE FED LET COMMERCIAL BANKS GO INTO THE BUSINESS OF SELLING SECURITIZED MORTGAGES IN A LIMITED WAY.

THUS COMMERCIAL AND INVESTMENT BANKS BEGAN TO OVERLAP. GLASS-STEAGALL BEGAN TO ERODE.

INVESTMENT BANK

COM-MERCIAL BANK

1996 THE FED LET THE HOLDING COMPANIES WHICH OWN COMMERCIAL BANKS OWN INVESTMENT BANKS TOO.

GLASS-STEAGALL DISINTEGRATED FURTHER.

INVESTMENT BANK

COMMERCIAL BANK

1997 CLINTON SIGNED THE TAXPAYER RELIEF ACT, LETTING HOMEOWNERS PAY NO TAXES ON PROFITS FROM THE SALE OF THEIR HOMES UP TO $500,000.

NOT JUST A HOME, AN INVESTMENT!

1999 FANNIE MAE LOOSENED CREDIT REQUIREMENTS ON MORTGAGES SHE BOUGHT. KNOWING THAT FANNIE WOULD BUY UP RISKY LOANS LED BANKS TO ISSUE THEM.

1999: THE REPUBLICAN CONGRESS PASSED, AND BILL CLINTON SIGNED, THE GRAMM-LEACH-BILEY BILL, WHICH COMPLETELY REPEALED THOSE PARTS OF GLASS-STEAGALL WHICH HAD SEPARATED COMMERCIAL BANKS, INVESTMENT HOUSES, AND INSURANCE COMPANIES FROM EACH OTHER.

2000 IN THE WANING DAYS OF THE CLINTON ADMINISTRATION, CONGRESS AND THE PRESIDENT PASSED THE COMMODITIES FUTURES MODERN-IZATION ACT.

MAKING IT HARDER TO REGULATE "DERIVATIVES" SUCH AS THE "CREDIT DEFAULT SWAPS" WHICH WERE SUPPOSED TO INSURE MBS's.

2004: THE SECURITIES AND EXCHANGE COMMISSION RELAXED ITS NET CAPITAL RULE. THIS MEANT INVESTMENT BANKS NO LONGER HAD TO KEEP ENOUGH MONEY ON HAND TO COVER THEIR LOSSES. THEY COULD NOW BORROW A VAST SUM OF MONEY AND INVEST IT AS THEY PLEASED.

WITHOUT THIS DEREGULATION IT WOULD NOT BE POSSIBLE FOR LEHMAN BROTHERS TO BORROW 30 TIMES MORE MONEY THAN THE COMPANY WAS WORTH AND INVEST IT IN RISKY MBS'S. BUSH LET BANKS BET BULLISHLY WITH BORROWED BUCKS.

WITH FDR'S REGULATIONS OUT OF THE WAY...

FDR – R.I.P.

THE TRADE IN MBS's BECAME EASIER, MORE PROFITABLE.

IT WAS NOW POSSIBLE FOR A COMMERCIAL BANK TO FULLY EXPLOIT THE MORTGAGE MARKET.

IT WAS THE BEGINING OF A HOUSING BOOM THAT WOULD LAST LESS THAN TEN YEARS.

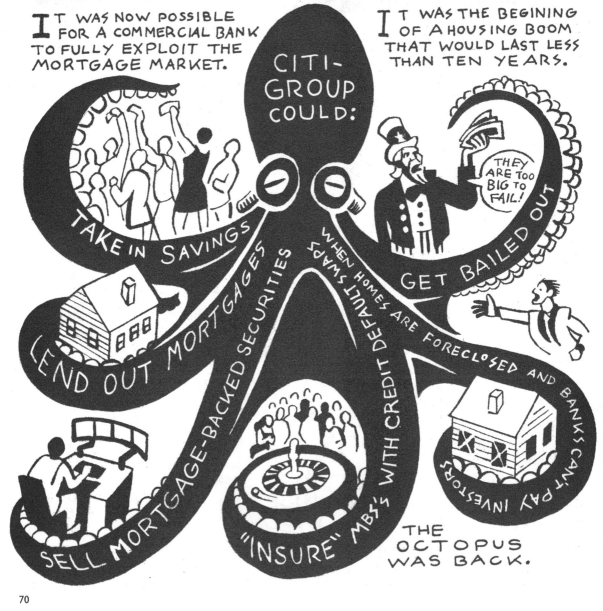

CITI-GROUP COULD:

TAKE IN SAVINGS

GET BAILED OUT

THEY ARE TOO BIG TO FAIL!

LEND OUT MORTGAGES

SELL MORTGAGE-BACKED SECURITIES

"INSURE" MBS's WITH CREDIT DEFAULT SWAPS

WHEN HOMES ARE FORECLOSED AND BANKS CAN'T PAY INVESTORS

THE OCTOPUS WAS BACK.

HOW DID THE U.S. BECOME A NATION OF DEBTORS?
FIGURING OUT TODAY'S ECONOMIC CRISIS REQUIRES A TRIP BACK TO THE '70s.

THE GREAT CRACKDOWN

MOST PEOPLE REMEMBER THE 1970s AS A TIME OF DISCO AND LEISURE SUITS, BUT THE ELITE WAS UNHAPPY.

ABROAD, THE U.S. HAD LOST THE VIETNAM WAR.

THE 3RD WORLD WAS IN REVOLT!

AT HOME, WORKERS HAD A BAD ATTITUDE,

SMOKE-ING POT ON THEIR COFFEE BREAKS AND SABOTAGING ASSEMBLY LINES.

POSTAL CARRIERS WENT ON STRIKE.

SOME THING MUST BE DONE.

CORPORATE PROFITS WERE WAY DOWN FROM THEIR 1950s & 1960s PEAKS. THE MARKETS PERFORMED MISER-ABLY.

TIME FOR A CRACK-DOWN!

VOLCKER INTENTIONALLY PROVOKED THE WORST RECESSION SINCE THE 1930S. ONE YEAR LATER AMERICANS, ANGRY ABOUT THE ECONOMY, VOTED OUT CARTER

AND ELECTED RONALD REAGAN.

REAGAN IMMEDIATELY LENT VOLCKER A HAND BY CUTTING TAXES ON THE RICH.

AND CUTTING SOCIAL SPENDING ON THE POOR.

IN AUGUST 1981, REAGAN FIRED THE STRIKING AIR TRAFFIC CONTROLLERS, WHOSE UNION HAD SUPPORTED HIS CAMPAIGN, SIGNALING OPEN SEASON FOR UNION BUSTING. THE CLASS WAR FROM ABOVE WAS UNDERWAY!

patco

THIS STRATEGY PRESENTED A PROBLEM!

HOW CAN AN ECONOMY DEPENDANT ON HIGH LEVELS OF CONSUMPTION, AND A POLITICAL SYSTEM WHOSE STABILITY REQUIRED AN ELECTORATE WELL-SUPPLIED WITH MATERIAL GOODS, COPE WITH AN ATTACK ON THE INCOME AND ECONOMIC SECURITY OF THE MAJORITY

THEIR ANSWER: WORK HARDER, BORROW MORE! FROM THE LATE 1970s TO THE EARLY 2000s, MORE PEOPLE JOINED THE WORKFORCE BUT THE AVERAGE WAGE STAYED LEVEL OR FELL. MEANWHILE, CONSUMPTION ROSE FROM 62% OF THE U.S. ECONOMY TO 71% IN 2008.

THIS COULD NOT HAVE HAPPENED WITHOUT THE MAGIC OF CREDIT.

VOLCKER, REAGAN, AND THE SHAREHOLDER REVOLUTION WERE HELL ON AMERICAN MANUFACTURING. THE 1980s RECESSION KILLED ABOUT 3 MILLION FACTORY JOBS. THE SECTOR NEVER RECOVERED. BETWEEN 1998 AND 2008 WE LOST ALMOST 5 MILLION FACTORY JOBS. THE LOSS OF AMERICAN MANUFACTURING MEANT THAT ALL THAT CONSUMPTION COULD ONLY BE SATISFIED BY IMPORTS SHIPPED IN FROM PLACES LIKE CHINA, WHOSE GOODS FILL THE SHELVES AT WALMART.

CHINA ★

THE ELITE LIKED THIS.

WAL★MART

CHEAP GOODS AT WALMART MADE IT EASY TO KEEP AMERICAN WAGES DOWN. NO WONDER WALMART STOCK ROSE 49,555% BETWEEN 1980 AND 1999.

BUT ALL THOSE IMPORTS CAME WITH A LONG-TERM COST. YOU CAN'T CONSUME MORE THAN YOU PRODUCE WITHOUT BORROWING LOTS OF MONEY. ALL THOSE DOLLARS WE WERE SHIPPING OFF TO CHINA, THE CHINESE LENT BACK TO US.

THIS HAD THE EFFECT OF RAISING THE VALUE OF THE DOLLAR, WHICH MADE IT HARD FOR AMERICAN LABOR TO COMPETE WITH FOREIGN WORKERS WHO WERE PAID IN CHEAPER CURRENCY.

A SAVINGS REFLECTED IN THE COST OF GOODS THEY PRODUCED AND SOLD TO US.

LOANS FROM CHINA HELPED FUEL OUR HOUSING BOOM. THE CENTRAL BANKS OF CHINA (AND JAPAN AND INDIA AND...) BOUGHT HUNDREDS OF BILLIONS OF DOLLARS IN BONDS FROM FANNIE MAE AND FREDDIE MAC.

中国人民银行

PEOPLE'S BANK OF CHINA

"ASIA LENDS, AMERICA SPENDS"

BUT THAT TRANSPACIFIC MERRY-GO-ROUND NOW LOOKS BROKEN BEYOND REPAIR. THE U.S. NOW OWES THE WORLD ALMOST $6 TRILLION, MORE THAN A TRILLION OF IT TO CHINA. BUT THE ONLY WAY OUR GOVERNMENT CAN THINK OF TO GET OUT OF THIS MESS IS TO BORROW MORE AND SPEND OURSELVES OUT OF ECONOMIC COLLAPSE.

ASIA LENDS ERIC SPEW

BAILOUT

HOW HAS THE U.S. GOVERNMENT RESPONDED TO THE FINANCIAL CRISIS?

BY JANUARY 2008 THE BUBBLE HAD BURST. HOUSE PRICES WERE PLUMMETING. BANKS WERE JACKING UP INTEREST RATES ON ARMS. FOLKS FOUND THEMSELVES "UNDERWATER"; THEIR HOMES SUDDENLY WORTH LESS THAN THE VALUE OF THEIR MORTGAGES. BUT BANKS STILL WANTED THEIR MONEY. WHEN THEY COULDN'T GET IT, THEY FORECLOSED. MORE THAN $4 TRILLION THAT PEOPLE HAD PUT IN THEIR HOMES HAD VAPORIZED. MANY WERE BANKRUPT. THEY LOOKED TO WASHINGTON FOR HELP.

BUT THE BANKS WERE HURTING TOO. WHEN THE HOUSING BUBBLE STARTED TO DEFLATE, BIG FIRMS LIKE LEHMAN BROTHERS, BEAR STEARNS, CITIGROUP AND BANK OF AMERICA COULDN'T BELIEVE IT. THEY THOUGHT THE MARKET WOULD COME BACK FAST. WHEN IT DIDN'T, BEAR STEARNS HAD TO SELL OUT AND LEHMAN CRASHED AND BURNED. THE OTHERS FOUND THEMSELVES TEETERING ON THE EDGE OF BANKRUPTCY. HOMEOWNERS NEEDED HELP. WALL STREET NEEDED HELP. WHO WOULD UNCLE SAM DECIDE TO RESCUE?

AFTER THE CRASH, CONGRESS AND THE WHITE HOUSE TALKED ABOUT MAKING FUNDAMENTAL REFORMS THAT WOULD KEEP THE SAME THING FROM HAPPENING AGAIN. BUT INSTEAD, THEY PATCHED UP THE OLD SYSTEM AND SENT IT BACK OUT, WITH ALL THE OLD RISKS, INEQUITIES, AND ABUSES. IT WASN'T A TRANSFORMATION. IT WAS A BAILOUT.

THE BAILOUT BEGAN ON OCTOBER 3, 2008, WHEN CONGRESS PASSED THE EMERGENCY ECONOMIC STABILIZATION ACT. IT AUTHORIZED THE GOVERNMENT TO USE $700 BILLION TO RESCUE THE NATION'S FINANCIAL SYSTEM. SOME MEMBERS OF CONGRESS WEREN'T SURE THEY LIKED WHAT THEY SAW. SHOULDN'T WE BE DOING SOMETHING TO RESCUE HOMEOWNERS TOO, NOT JUST BANKERS WHO HAD SLIPPED ON THEIR OWN MESS? TREASURY SECRETARY HENRY PAULSON BROWBEAT THEM INTO PASSING THE BILL, WARNING THAT IF THEY DIDN'T, THE CRASH COULD LEAD TO POPULAR PANIC REQUIRING MARTIAL LAW TO PUT DOWN.

THE IDEA BEHIND THE BAILOUT WAS THAT IF BANKS RECEIVED MONEY TO COVER THEIR LOSSES, THEY WOULD KEEP MAKING LOANS NECESSARY TO KEEP THE ECONOMY GOING.

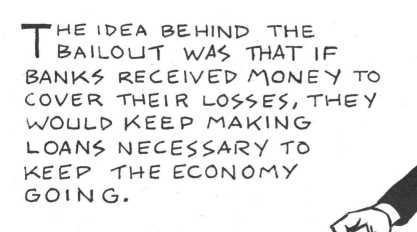

BUT THIS BAILOUT CAME WITH NO STRINGS ATTACHED. BANKS WERE NOT REQUIRED TO MAKE THOSE LOANS.

THE TREASURY STARTED TO PUMP MONEY INTO BANKS IT CONSIDERED "TOO BIG TO FAIL." THE PROGRAM WAS CALLED THE TROUBLED ASSET RELIEF PROGRAM, OR TARP.

THE GOVERNMENT
GAVE THE BANKS A
VERY TASTY DEAL.
WHEN AIG, THE WORLD'S
LARGEST INSURANCE
COMPANY, WAS ON THE
VERGE OF COLLAPSE,
THE GOVERNMENT
TOOK IT OVER.
INSTEAD OF ASKING
ITS CREDITORS, BIG
INVESTMENT BANKS,
TO TAKE A LOSS
ON THEIR LOANS,
THE FED AGREED TO
PAY THEM OFF IN
FULL: A $65 BILLION
GIFT FROM THE
TAXPAYERS TO
THE BANKS.

UNDER OBAMA THE BAILOUT GREW EVEN LARGER.

ONE OF THE KEY PROBLEMS THE ECONOMY FACES IS
THAT BANKS ARE SO LOADED DOWN WITH BAD LOANS
THAT THEY HAVE A HARD TIME MAKING NEW LOANS.

OBAMA ADDED PROGRAMS THAT WERE SUPPOSED TO
SOLVE THIS PROBLEM BY BUYING UP BAD DEBT
HELD BY THE BANKS, THUS CLEANING UP THE BANKS'
BOOKS. BUYING UP BAD MORTGAGES HELD BY THOSE
BANKS WOULD ALSO KEEP HOUSE PRICES FROM FALLING.

THE OBAMA ADMINISTRATION WAS MAKING A HUGE
BET ON BEHALF OF THE TAXPAYERS
THAT THESE ASSETS WERE JUST
TEMPORARILY UNDERVALUED.

IF THEY WERE WRONG, THE GOVERNMENT
COULD LOSE A LOT OF MONEY.

THE FED ALLOWED BANKS WITH MORE THAN $100 BILLION IN ASSETS TO BORROW MONEY AT LOWER INTEREST RATES THAN SMALLER BANKS. REGULATORS BENT RULES SO THAT BIG BANKS LIKE J.P. MORGAN CHASE, WELLS FARGO, AND BANK OF AMERICA COULD HOLD A LARGER SHARE OF BANK DEPOSITS IN SOME METROPOLITAN AREAS THAN THE LEGAL LIMIT. THESE POLICIES, ALONG WITH THE NOTION THAT THESE COMPANIES WERE "TOO BIG TO FAIL," LET A SMALL NUMBER OF BANKS TAKE OVER. WHEN THE DUST CLEARS, THERE WILL BE FEWER BANKS AND THEY WILL BE FAR MORE POWERFUL.

THE BAILOUT DIDN'T GET BANKS BACK TO LENDING MONEY. THEY DIDN'T HAVE TO. THEY WERE MAKING MONEY THE EASY WAY. THE FED WAS ALLOWING THEM TO BORROW MONEY AT INCREDIBLY LOW RATES WHICH THEY THEN USED TO SPECULATE IN THE SAME RISKY WAYS.

LOBBYISTS FOR THE BANKS WERE BUYING OFF ELECTED OFFICIALS. THEIR AIM: TO HALT ANY RESTRICTIONS ON THE BUSINESS PRACTICES THAT HAD LED TO THE CRASH.

THE AVERAGE HOMEOWNER, ON THE OTHER HAND, WAS IN NO POSITION TO BUY POLITICAL INFLUENCE.

ONE WAY TO HELP THE ECONOMY WOULD HAVE BEEN TO MAKE HOMEOWNERSHIP AFFORDABLE AGAIN. BUT WASHINGTON WASN'T INTERESTED.

INSTEAD OF HELPING HOMEOWNERS DIRECTLY, WASHINGTON TRIED TO BRIBE THE BANKS INTO HELPING THEM. THE HOPE FOR HOMEOWNERS PROGRAM, LAUNCHED IN 2008, OFFERED BANKS INCENTIVES TO MODIFY MORTGAGES. AFTER 9 MONTHS, ONLY 51 HOMES HAD BEEN SAVED THIS WAY.

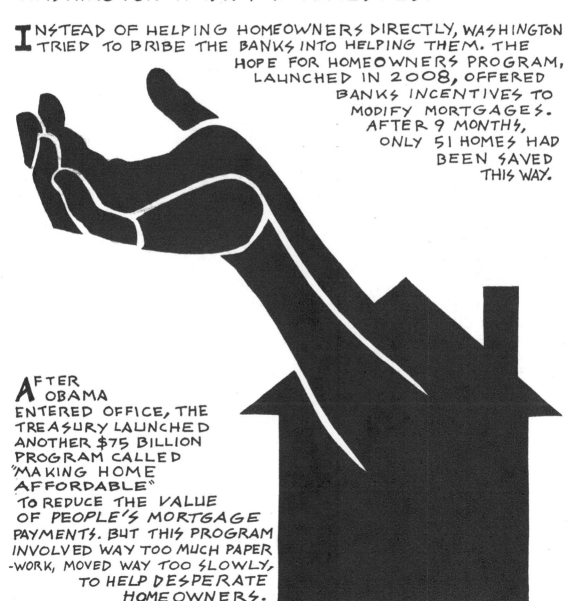

AFTER OBAMA ENTERED OFFICE, THE TREASURY LAUNCHED ANOTHER $75 BILLION PROGRAM CALLED "MAKING HOME AFFORDABLE" TO REDUCE THE VALUE OF PEOPLE'S MORTGAGE PAYMENTS. BUT THIS PROGRAM INVOLVED WAY TOO MUCH PAPER-WORK, MOVED WAY TOO SLOWLY, TO HELP DESPERATE HOMEOWNERS.

MEANWHILE, THE FINANCIAL SECTOR WAS DOING FINE. IN 2009, EMPLOYEES OF MAJOR U.S. BANKS SET A NEW RECORD FOR COMPENSATION.

BUT THE REAL ECONOMY, THE VAST MAJORITY OF AMERICANS WHO DIDN'T WORK ON WALL STREET, WERE STILL IN CRISIS.

THE POOR WERE THE HARDEST HIT. THEY DEPEND ON MEDICAID, WORKERS COMP AND OTHER PROGRAMS ADMINISTERED BY THE STATES. AFTER THE CRASH, STATES' TAX REVENUES FELL. SO CONGRESS PASSED A $787 BILLION STIMULUS BILL, GIVING PART OF IT TO THE STATES. BUT THIS WAS NOT ENOUGH.

WHAT CAN THE GOVERNMENT DO TO HELP ORDINARY PEOPLE RECOVER AND TO PREVENT ANOTHER CRASH?

YEAH!

THE ECONOMY IS COMING BACK!

AND I LIKE IT!

SPEAK FOR YOURSELF.

INSTEAD OF BAILING OUT THE BANKS, DO SOMETHING FOR THE PEOPLE.

A ONE-YEAR MORATORIUM ON FORECLOSURES WOULD BE A START. THE GOVERNMENT COULD PROVIDE LOW-INTEREST LOANS TO FOLKS FACING FORECLOSURE. BUT IN THE LONG RUN THE BANKS SHOULD BE FORCED TO RENEGOTIATE MORTGAGES—OR JUST FORGIVE DEBTS.

PEOPLE NEED HIGHER WAGES. THE GOVERNMENT COULD ABOLISH LAWS THAT MAKE IT HARD FOR UNIONS TO ORGANIZE. AND IT COULD RENEGOTIATE OR CANCEL TRADE TREATIES THAT ENCOURAGE OUTSOURCING.

UNEMPLOYMENT INSURANCE NEEDS TO BE EXPANDED AND MODERNIZED TO SAVE HOUSEHOLDS FROM POVERTY.

ONE OF THE BIGGEST CAUSES OF HOUSEHOLD DEBT IS THE COST OF HEALTH CARE. WE SHOULD GET RID OF A MEDICAL SYSTEM DOMINATED BY THE PRIVATE HEALTH INSURANCE INDUSTRY AND REPLACE IT WITH A SINGLE PAYER SYSTEM.

AS FOR THOSE WHO DID THIS TO US:

WHAT CAN BE DONE TO REIN IN THE FINANCIAL SECTOR?

THE RESTRICTIONS OF GLASS-STEAGALL SHOULD BE BROUGHT BACK.

CREDIT DEFAULT SWAPS SHOULD BE BANNED.

FANNIE MAE AND FREDDIE MAC SHOULD BE RECONSTITUTED AS GOVERNMENT-RUN AGENCIES, THAT WAY THEY CAN STICK TO THEIR JOB OF HELPING PEOPLE GET MORTGAGES.

BUT HOW TO STOP ANOTHER BUBBLE FROM FORMING?

A TAX ON STOCK AND BOND TRANSACTIONS WOULD ENCOURAGE INVESTORS TO TRADE ONLY WHEN THEY WANT TO MAKE LONG-TERM INVESTMENTS RATHER THAN SPECULATING.

Could we have financial regulatory agencies that actually regulate finance?

Some, like the SEC and the CFTC, need better funding and greater authority to investigate and prosecute white-collar criminals in the financial sector.

But the federal reserve is the biggest and most powerful of these agencies. It's too much under the control of banks, so it has no incentive to stop them when they get reckless. Congress should either take control of the Fed away from the banks or give its regulatory duties to a separate agency.

It's clear there needs to be better regulation of all financial products sold to individuals, from mortgages to mutual funds.

The more complicated the products, the more closely regulators should look at them —

AND THERE SHOULD BE MORE SEVERE PENALTIES IF THEY PROVE TO BE DECEPTIVE.

WE'VE SHOWN HERE THAT THERE IS A LOT THE GOVERNMENT COULD BE DOING TO GET US OUT OF THIS CRISIS AND PREVENT ANOTHER ONE. BUT IT'S NOT LIKELY THAT TOMORROW MORNING ELECTED OFFICIALS WILL WAKE UP AND DECIDE TO DO THE RIGHT THING. BECAUSE IN WASHINGTON, WALL STREET SPEAKS LOUDER THAN MAIN STREET. WE HAVE A GOVERNMENT OF, BY, AND FOR THE WEALTHY.

AND THIS IS NOT GOING TO CHANGE UNTIL THOSE OF US ON MAIN STREET START TO MAKE SOME NOISE.

WE NEED

A MILITANT
MASS MOVEMENT
AGAINST THE BANKS
AND BIG BUSINESS.

BUILDING A MOVEMENT STARTS WITH PEOPLE ADDRESSING THE CAUSE OF THE PROBLEM. THE ECONOMIC CRISIS IS PARTLY THE RESULT OF REAL ESTATE SPECULATION. IN OTHER WORDS, IT IS THE RESULT OF PEOPLE BUYING HOUSES, NOT TO LIVE IN THEM BUT TO SELL THEM AT A PROFIT. SOME SAY THAT IS THE AMERICAN WAY, BUT THERE HAVE ALWAYS BEEN AMERICANS WHO DID NOT AGREE.

THIS LAND IS OUR LAND

ONE DOES NOT SELL THE LAND PEOPLE WALK ON.

CRAZY HORSE, 1875

WHENEVER THERE IS IN ANY COUNTRY UNCULTIVATED LANDS AND UNEMPLOYED POOR IT IS CLEAR THAT THE LAWS OF PROPERTY HAVE BEEN SO FAR EXTENDED AS TO VIOLATE NATURAL RIGHTS.

THE EARTH IS GIVEN AS A COMMON STOCK FOR MAN TO LABOR AND LIVE ON.

THOMAS JEFFERSON 1785

DURING THE GREAT DEPRESSION, MANY FOLKS COULD NOT PAY THEIR RENT. LANDLORDS SENT MEN TO EVICT TENANTS,

THE LANDLORDS' MEN WOULD CARRY OUT THE TENANTS' FURNITURE, THEN CHANGE THE LOCKS ON THEIR DOORS...

LEAVING TENANTS ON THE STREET.

UNTIL NEIGHBORS CAME BY AND OFFERED TO HELP.

THE NEIGHBORS WOULD BREAK THE LOCKS AND CARRY THE FURNITURE BACK INSIDE.

SOME-TIMES EVICTION RESISTANCE RESULTED IN PEOPLE KEEPING THEIR HOMES.

SOMETIMES RESISTANCE CAUSED RIOTS.

THESE STRUGGLES LED TO REFORMS SUCH AS PUBLIC HOUSING AND RENT CONTROL. ROOSEVELT'S NEW DEAL WAS THE RESULT OF A MILITANT MASS MOVEMENT. IS SUCH A MOVEMENT POSSIBLE TODAY?

RENT STRIKE

INDIVIDUALISM SEEMS TO BE AN OBSTACLE TO BUILDING A MOVEMENT. "WE HAVE A LOT OF DENIAL. THE MENTALITY HAS BEEN, 'STAY OUT OF MY BUSINESS. I DON'T WANT ANYBODY TO KNOW WHAT'S GOING ON.' EVERYBODY WANTED A PIECE OF THAT AMERICAN DREAM AND THEY DON'T WANT ANYONE TO KNOW THEY CAN'T HANDLE IT. UNTIL THE SHERIFF IS KNOCKING AT THEIR DOOR." THE WORDS OF BENIE HOPKINS OF CLEVELAND'S UNION MILES DEVELOPMENT CORPORATION.

IN A CONVERTED CLEVELAND FACTORY BUILDING, PEOPLE ARE TRYING TO PREVENT FORECLOSURES.

THESE ARE THE OFFICES OF THE EAST SIDE ORGANIZING PROJECT (ESOP).

TWICE A DAY, HOMEOWNERS FILE IN FOR A MEETING.

THE MEETING BEGINS WITH FILLING OUT FORMS. IT USED TO BE THAT MOST OF THE FOLKS WHO CAME TO ESOP FOR HELP WERE BLACK, BUT THERE ARE MORE AND MORE SUBURBAN WHITES. THIS RECESSION IS GETTING DEEPER.

THEY ALL FEAR LOSING THEIR HOME.

ESOP HAS BEEN AROUND SINCE THE '90S. WE ARE COMMUNITY ORGANIZERS. SINCE 2001 OUR PRIMARY FOCUS

HAS BEEN THIS HOUSING CRISIS,

BECAUSE SO MANY OF THE FOLKS WE WORKED WITH ON OTHER ISSUES WERE RAISING THE ISSUE OF THEIR HOME LOANS BEING A PROBLEM.

MANY FOLKS WERE INVOLVED IN LOAN PRODUCTS THAT WERE DESIGNED TO FAIL. COUNTRYWIDE WAS THE LARGEST PURVEYOR OF SUCH LOANS.

HOMEOWNERS AND ACTIVISTS OCCUPIED THE LOCAL OFFICE OF COUNTRYWIDE!

COUNTRYWIDE ARE LOAN SHARKS

POLICE AND REPORTERS SHOWED UP.

POLICE NEED A RAISE!

COUNTRY ARE LO

THIS SOUNDS REASONABLE.

GIVE THESE PEOPLE A BREAK.

WE EVENTUALLY ENTERED INTO NEGOTIATIONS WITH COUNTRYWIDE (AND OTHER BANKS) TO MODIFY PEOPLE'S MORTGAGES.

AND DON'T CALL US LOAN SHARKS.

ONCE BANKS SIT DOWN WITH US, THEY SEE WE ARE ON THE SAME PAGE. WE'RE ASKING THEM TO GIVE A RESPONSIBLE BORROWER A RESPONSIBLE PRODUCT.

WE ARE SUCCESSFUL AT SAVING THE HOMES OF 75% OF THE FOLKS WE REPRESENT.

THEN THE MEETING BREAKS INTO MANY SMALL MEETINGS AS FAMILIES TALK TO ESOP ACTIVISTS, EXPLAINING THEIR SITUATIONS, LOOKING FOR A WAY TO RENEGOTIATE THEIR MORTGAGES. THIS METHOD HAS SAVED MANY HOMES.

BUT IT DOES SEEM TO LET THE LOAN SHARKS OFF THE HOOK.

IN MIAMI TODAY A MORE MILITANT METHOD IS BEING TRIED.

MARY TRODY WEARS A PICTURE OF HER SON (WHO DIED IN AN ACCIDENT WHILE WORKING AS A SECURITY GUARD) ON HER CHEST,

AND HER WHOLE MULTI-RACIAL FAMILY ON HER BACK!

We Love You

12 OF THEM, 4 GENERATIONS OF HER FAMILY, LIVED TOGETHER IN A LITTLE HOUSE OWNED BY HER MOM.

WHEN HER HUSBAND LOST HIS JOB, SHE BECAME THE BREADWINNER, DELIVERING PAPERS OUT OF THE FAMILY TRUCK.

SO MARY HAD TO PAY FOR GAS AND INSURANCE.

THEY HAD TO TAKE A 2ND MORTGAGE AGAINST THE HOUSE. THEY SOON FOUND THEY COULD NOT PAY IT BACK. SO ONE DAY MARY DISCOVERED A 3-DAY NOTICE OF EVICTION TAPED TO HER DOOR!

THAT FRIDAY THE TRODYS MOVED OUT.

SHELTERS IN MIAMI DON'T TAKE FAMILIES.

SO THE TRODY FAMILY HAD TO SLEEP IN THE TRUCK THAT WEEKEND. THEY WATCHED A SPEECH BY THE PRESIDENT FROM THERE.

BUT MARY WAS NO VICTIM. SHE WAS A MEMBER OF LIFFT (LOW INCOME FAMILIES FIGHTING TOGETHER).

LIFFT

L.IFFT

THE VAN HAD BEEN USED FOR VOTER REGISTRATION...

CHANGE

AND HAD LED MIAMI'S OBAMA VICTORY PARADE.

OBAMA

OBAMA

SO MARY KNEW TO GO TO LIFFT WITH HER PROBLEM. THEY REFERRED HER TO MAX RAMEAU FROM TAKE BACK THE LAND, A GROUP THAT FIGHTS FOR THE HOMELESS.

TAKE BACK THE

LIFFT

THAT REAL ESTATE AGENT MAY NOT HAVE CARED, BUT OTHER PEOPLE SURE DID. COPS CAME. ALONG WITH A BARRACUDA FROM THE BANK.

A TENSE STANDOFF ENSUED.

TAKE BACK THE LAND

POWER U

COULD YOU GET YOUR SON OUT OF THERE? WE DON'T WANT TO ARREST A MINOR.

BUT THE BOY WOULD NOT LEAVE HIS HOME.

IN THE END, THE COPS BACKED OFF...

AND DROVE AWAY.

< / FFT

THE TRODYS MOVED BACK INTO THAT HOUSE. THEY ARE STILL THERE.

MARY'S DAUGHTER IS A FRESHMAN AT EVEREST COLLEGE AND A MOTHER OF FOUR. SHE SAYS MOVING BACK IN WASN'T EASY.

IT WAS STILL THE SAME AS IT WAS LIVING IN THE TRUCK BECAUSE THE FIRST COUPLE DAYS I COULDN'T GET ANY SLEEP. I WAS WORRIED. I CAN'T SLEEP. I HAVE TO SIT THERE AND WATCH MY KIDS SLEEP AND MAKE SURE THEY'RE OK! I COULDN'T SLEEP FOR A WHOLE WEEK STRAIGHT!

THAT'S WHY I HAVEN'T BEEN GOING TO SCHOOL LATELY. I HAVE TO MAKE SURE EVERY-THING IS STABLE BEFORE I GO BACK TO SCHOOL. TO FINISH MY CLASSES I'LL HAVE TO BE FOCUSED ON THAT.

FOR THE TRODY FAMILY, THE STRUGGLE ISN'T OVER.

BUT TAKE BACK THE LAND ISN'T JUST PUTTING HOMEOWNERS BACK IN THEIR HOMES. THEIR PRIMARY FOCUS IS HOMELESSNESS. THEIR TACTIC IS MOVING THE HOMELESS INTO FORECLOSED HOUSES.

NOT EVERYONE THINKS THIS IS A GREAT IDEA.

THE NUMBER OF PEOPLE STAYING IN CLEVELAND'S SHELTERS WENT DOWN THIS YEAR. BUT THE NUMBER OF HOUSE FIRES SKYROCKETED. FOLKS ARE GOING INTO THESE EMPTY HOUSES. THEY'RE SQUATTING. IT'S NOT SAFE. A LOT OF THEM ARE DRUG DEALERS. SOMEONE GETS COLD, THEY SET A FIRE, IT GETS OUT OF CONTROL!

TO PREVENT PROBLEMS, TAKE BACK THE LAND HAS STRICT GUIDELINES.

HOUSES MUST BE FORECLOSED OR GOVERNMENT-OWNED, NOT PRIVATE. MUST BE IN GOOD SHAPE, NO LEAKY ROOFS. NO HOLES IN FLOORBOARDS. MUST HAVE THE CAPACITY TO HAVE WATER AND ELECTRICITY.

WE DO FAMILIES, NOT INDIVIDUALS. FAMILIES MUST WORK ON FIXING UP THE HOMES. THEY MUST KEEP ELECTRICITY AND WATER ON. THEY HAVE TO BE GOOD NEIGHBORS. IF THEY HAVE A PROBLEM THAT KEEPS THEM FROM BEING A GOOD NEIGHBOR, SUCH AS DRUGS OR SEVERE MENTAL ILLNESS, THEN WE WON'T MOVE THEM IN.

SO FAR, MIAMI POLICE HAVE DONE LITTLE OR NOTHING TO STOP TAKE BACK THE LAND FROM SEIZING HOUSES.

WHAT SOCIAL GOOD WOULD BE SERVED BY ARRESTING A MOTHER AND SEPARATING HER FROM HER CHILDREN?

CHIEF TIMONEY

THERE IS A SMALL GROUP OF PEOPLE RESPONSIBLE FOR THIS ECONOMIC MELTDOWN. THOSE PEOPLE HAVEN'T BEEN ARRESTED. POLICE WOULD PUT THEMSELVES IN AN ODD POSITION IF THEY ARE NOT ARRESTING THOSE RESPONSIBLE FOR THE HOUSING CRISIS, BUT THEN ARREST PEOPLE WHO ARE TRYING TO SOLVE THAT CRISIS. I THINK POLICE LOOK AT THAT AND SAY "WE CAN'T DO THIS. PUBLIC SENTIMENT WOULD TURN AGAINST US."

TO CHARGE A SQUATTER WITH TRESPASSING, THE OWNER MUST COMPLAIN THAT SOMEONE IS ON THEIR PROPERTY WHO SHOULDN'T BE. IF THE OWNER IS A NON-HUMAN BEING IN ANOTHER STATE, HOW DOES THAT ENTITY MAKE A COMPLAINT TO THE POLICE? MANY OF THESE HOMES HAVE SECURITIZED MORTGAGES. THEY'RE OWNED BY A BUNCH OF INVESTORS. THE RETIREMENT FUND FOR THE MIAMI SCHOOL SYSTEM INVESTS IN MORTGAGE BACKED SECURITIES. 10,000 TEACHERS EACH OWN A PIECE OF 50 HOUSES. SO, DO THE POLICE CALL 10,000 TEACHERS AND ASK THEM, "DO YOU WANT THIS GUY HERE?"

TAKE BACK

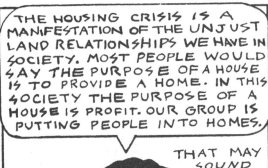

THE HOUSING CRISIS IS A MANIFESTATION OF THE UNJUST LAND RELATIONSHIPS WE HAVE IN SOCIETY. MOST PEOPLE WOULD SAY THE PURPOSE OF A HOUSE IS TO PROVIDE A HOME. IN THIS SOCIETY THE PURPOSE OF A HOUSE IS PROFIT. OUR GROUP IS PUTTING PEOPLE INTO HOMES.

THAT MAY SOUND RADICAL, BUT CHECK THIS OUT.

OHIO CONGRESSWOMAN MARCY KAPTUR HAS TOLD HOMEOWNERS IN FORECLOSURE TO RESIST EVICTION.

...DO NOT LEAVE YOUR HOME. BECAUSE, REMEMBER POSSESSION IS 90% OF THE LAW.

IF POLITICIANS AND POLICE ARE STARTING TO SEE SENSE IN SQUATTING, MAYBE "THE LAWS OF PROPERTY" REALLY "HAVE BEEN SO FAR EXTENDED AS TO VIOLATE NATURAL RIGHTS." MAYBE IT'S TIME TO REEXAMINE HOW WE DEAL WITH THIS LAND OF OURS.

FACED WITH THE GREAT DEPRESSION, AMERICANS FOUGHT BACK AGAINST BIG CORPORATIONS WHO HAD WRECKED THE ECONOMY. THEY WON REFORMS THAT LED TO A GENERATION OF PROSPERITY. WE SHOULD DO NO LESS.

THIS LAND IS OUR LAND

FURTHER READING

Articles and Reports:

The housing bubble and the mortgage-fueled financial and economic collapse that followed caught America's mainstream journalists napping. Very few acknowledged that a bubble existed or understood the full implications when the Crash came. Since then, however, some outstanding reporting has appeared that analyzes the causes of the crisis and exposes the abuses that made it so severe. Almost all the articles below are available online.

Dean Baker and David Rosnick, "The Housing Crash and the Retirement Prospects of Late Baby Boomers," Center for Economic and Policy Research, June 2008.

Alex Blumberg and Adam Davidson, "The Giant Pool of Money," aired May 9, 2008, on Chicago Public Radio's "This American Life"; transcript available at http://www.thislife.org/Radio_Episode.aspx?episode=355.

Brady Dennis and Robert O'Harrow Jr, three-part *Washington Post* series on the collapse and bailout of AIG: "The Beautiful Machine," December 28, 2008; "A Crack in the System," December 30, 2008; and "Downgrades and Downfall," December 31, 2008.

Thomas B. Edsall, "Crony Capitalism: How the Financial Industry Gets What It Wants," *Huffington Post*, May 11, 2009.

James K. Galbraith, "No Return to Normal: Why the Economic Crisis, and Its Solutions, Are Bigger Than You Think," *Washington Monthly*, March–April 2009.

Peter S. Goodman, "Cashing In, Again, on Risky Mortgages: Suprime Brokers Resurface as Dubious Loan Fixers," *New York Times*, July 20, 2009.

Peter S. Goodman, "Foreclosures Force Ex-Homeowners to Turn to Shelters," *New York Times*, October 18, 2009.

William Greider, "Dismantling the Temple," *The Nation*, July 15, 2009.

Simon Johnson, "The Quiet Coup," *The Atlantic*, May 2009.

Andy Kroll, "The Greatest Swindle Ever Sold," *Mother Jones*, May 26, 2009.

Michael Lewis, "The End," *Condé Nast Portfolio*, November 11, 2008.

Gretchen Morgenson and Don Van Natta Jr., "Even in Crisis, Banks Dig in For Battle Against Regulation," *New York Times*, June 1, 2009.

Nomi Prins, "The Big Bank Bailout Payback Bamboozle," *Mother Jones*, June 14, 2009.

ProPublica, "History of U.S. Gov't Bailouts," April 15, 2009, http://www .propublica.org/special/government-bailouts.

Jack Rasmus, "Obama's Economic Plan vs. an Alternative," *Z Magazine*, March 2009.

Matthew Sherman, "A Short History of Financial Deregulation in the United States," Center for Economic and Policy Research, July 2009.

Matt Taibbi, "The Big Takeover," *Rolling Stone*, Issue 1075, April 2, 2009.

Books about the Crash:

Dean Baker, *Plunder and Blunder: The Rise and Fall of the Bubble Economy* (San Francisco: Polipoint Press, 2009)

William D. Cohan, *House of Cards: A Tale of Hubris and Wretched Excess on Wall Street* (New York: Doubleday, 2009)

David Wessel, *In Fed We Trust: Ben Bernanke's War on the Great Panic* (New York: Crown Business, 2009)

For Deeper Background:

Liaquat Ahamed, *Lords of Finance: The Bankers Who Broke the World* (New York: Penguin, 2009)

William Greider, *Secrets of the Temple: How the Federal Reserve Runs the Country* (New York: Simon and Schuster, 1987)

Doug Henwood, *Wall Street,* Updated Edition (New York: Verso, 1998)

Elizabeth Warren and Amelia Warren Tyagi, *The Two-Income Trap: Why Middle-Class Mothers and Fathers Are Going Broke* (New York: Basic Books, 2003)

ACKNOWLEDGMENTS

Special thanks to Laird Ogden and Tamara Tornado for inking "Bailout," and to William Ibanez for inking "Cruel Boom." We could not have stayed on track without you all.

Another special thanks to Doug Henwood for contributing "The Great Crackdown" and for his insightful foreword.

Seth Tobocman would like to acknowledge the many people and organizations who helped with research for this book:

In Cleveland: Marylin Tobocman, Edward G. Kramer of Housing Advocates Inc., Mrs. Redrick, everyone at the East Side Organizing Project, Benie Hopkins of the Union-Miles Development Corporation, Mark Wiseman of the Foreclosure Prevention Program.

In Miami: Paul Whalen, Harold Dodt, Joseph Phelan, Max Rameau of Take Back the Land, and his partner, Bernadette Armand. Mary Trody and her whole family. Ms. Cora, Denise Perry, everyone at the Miami Workers Center, LIFFT and Power U., Alan Farago (even though I didn't get to use as much of his information as I would have liked to).

In New York: Doug Henwood, Erin Sickler, Melissa Jamesson and the Museum of American Finance.

Seth Tobocman would also like to thank Peter Kuper for good advice. Art models Louisa Krupp, Blkangl Bradshaw, Sandy Aldrich, Tamarra, Stuart, and Junior.

Mumia Abu-Jamal for his ongoing support. And Francis Goldin and Sam Stoloff, who made this book happen.

Also Louisa Krupp; Tamarra Wydham; Edith, Bill, and Sarah Tobocman, all of whom were very tolerant of his absence from their lives while he worked on this book.

Eric Laursen thanks Seth Tobocman for pulling this project together; Jessica Wehrle for her extraordinary hard work and commitment; Sam Stoloff at the Frances Goldin Literary Agency for his hard work, assistance, and support; Soft Skull Press and particularly Denise Oswald for their enthusiastic commitment; and, as always, Mary V. Dearborn. Special thanks to Dean Baker for his comments and always useful critiques.

Jess Wehrle would like to thank: William, Laird, and Tamara (without you three, my hand and/or brain would probably have been crippled!), Ian for the love and not yelling too much about all the ink I've gotten on the kitchen table, Carolina for the friendship and the brushes used to make this book, Brian for taking a swell picture of my mug, Steven and ABC No Rio for generously letting us use the computer lab, Artie for being a comic nerd, Luisa for the adventures, Aubrie for all the friendship, all my families, and everyone who spent their hard-earned cash to buy this book.